TAKING PHOTOGRAPHS

Tessa Codrington

MEREHURST

ACKNOWLEDGEMENTS

The author and publishers would like to thank the following for their help during the course of producing this book: Stuart, Sarah Rose, Jacquetta and Charlotte Wheeler; Gareth, Jules, Josh and Sydney Robson; Naima and Benjamin Kelly; Brian Morris; Alexandra, Natasha, Tania and Rosie Llewellyn; Oliver Stephens; Dimitri Galitiine; Sarah Haslett; Rosie Thurgood; Valerie Davis; Jonathon Harvey; Samantha Turner; Tamara Lewis; Lucy Clarke; Ally Aitken; Anna; Angela; the Mills family; Deborah and Gavin Trott; the pupils of Macaulay School; Kodak Ltd; Fisher Price Ltd; Nikon Ltd; Polaroid Ltd.

Published 1995 by Merehurst Limited
Ferry House, 51-57 Lacy Road,
Putney, London SW15 IPR

© Copyright 1995 Tessa Codrington
ISBN 1898018 50 2

All rights reserved.

A catalogue for this book is available from the British Library.

Project Editor: Cheryl Brown
Designer: Anita Ruddell
Colour separation by Global Colour Malaysia
Produced by Mandarin Offset Ltd.
Printed in Hong Kong

CONTENTS

Click!	4
What Makes a Good Photograph?	6
Which Camera?	8
Using a Camera	10
Which Film?	12
Composing a Photograph	14
Lighting a Photograph	18
Using Flash	22
Common Mistakes	24
Out in the Country	26
A Day at the Beach	28
Out and About in the Town	30
Photographing a Person	32
Group Photographs	36
Photographing School Friends	38
Trick Photos	40
Photographing Animals	42
Action!	44
What Next?	46
Glossary	47
Index	48

CLICK!

Before cameras were invented, people who wanted to record a special day, or a person, or a beautiful scene, had to be able to draw or paint well. Now, in much the same way that we can travel in a day thousands of miles that in the past would have taken a whole lifetime, we can capture in a few minutes 36 pictures on a roll of film that would have taken days and days of artistic skill to reproduce. How lucky we are! We can just pick up a camera, make sure that it has got some film in it, take off the lens cap, point it at whatever we want to take a photograph of, and shoot.

THREE GOLDEN RULES

1 Take your camera with you wherever you go – shopping in the town, on a walk in the country, even when you're doing nothing in particular with your friends.

2 If you can't decide whether to take a picture or not, TAKE IT! At best you just might get a wonderful surprise, at worst you can always learn from your mistakes.

3 Always carry an extra roll of film and spare battery with you in your pocket wherever you go.

WHAT MAKES A GOOD PHOTOGRAPH?

Why are so many people disappointed when they get their photographs back from the film processors? The answer is that to take a good photograph you need to do a little bit more than simply aim your camera at a scene and press a button.

AT THE BEACH...

... IN THE TOWN

... OR AT HOME

You need to think first. You should try to imagine the picture you would like to take and then try to recreate that image in your photograph. To do this you will need to think about how to arrange the things in your photograph and the affect lighting will have on your picture. You will also need to know how to avoid the most common mistakes made by people when taking photographs. This book will show you all of these things and more so that you can produce successful photographs whatever the occasion and in any situation.

PHOTOGRAPHING A PERSON...

...OR A
GROUP OF
PEOPLE

PHOTOGRAPHING PEOPLE
WITH THEIR PETS...

...OR ANIMALS
ON THEIR
OWN

RECORDING SPECIAL
OCCASIONS...

...AND CELEBRATIONS

WHICH CAMERA?

There are a wide range of cameras available today. The information on these two pages will help you to decide which is the right one for you.

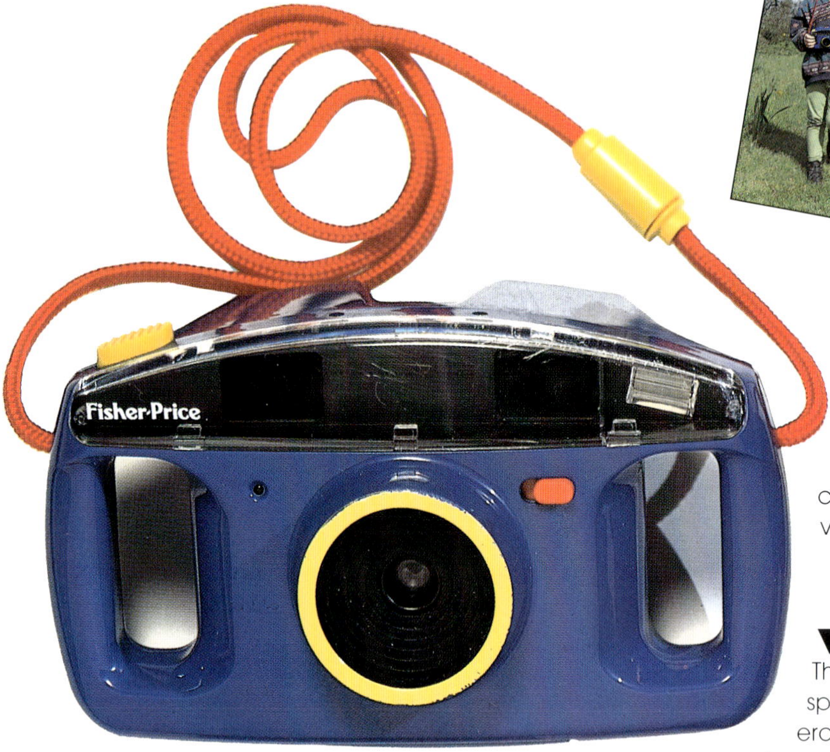

◄ A FIRST CAMERA
This camera is ideal for the very young photographer. It has two handles for a steady grip, and a sturdy plastic body. It uses 110 cartridge film (see page 12) which is very easy to load.

▼ AN AUTOMATIC CHOICE
The more money you can afford to spend on your 35 mm compact camera the more it will do for you. It will focus for you; it will turn on the flash if there is not enough light; it will wind on the film automatically between shots; and it will even rewind the film once it has been used up. An automatic camera may not have all these features, so do check before buying one what you are getting for your money. You should be able to buy a fully automatic camera for between £80 and £100.

AUTOMATIC JARGON
What can your automatic camera do for you?
Auto Exposure: The camera will make sure that the exposure (see page 18) is just right. This means that your photographs are not too light in bright light, and not too dark in poor light.
Auto Focus: The camera will take sharp pictures from close up (see manufacturer's instruction booklet for minimum distance).
Auto Flash: The camera will turn on the flash when there is not enough light.
Auto Wind: Each time you take a photograph the camera will wind on to the next frame of film for you.
Auto Rewind: When you have finished the film, the camera will rewind the film into the cassette.

▶ FIXED FOCUS

This is a fixed focus 35 mm compact camera. With this type of camera you must stand at least 1.5 metres from the object you want to photograph otherwise it will look all blurry. When buying a fixed focus camera do make sure that it has a built-in flash – the very cheapest don't and these will not take very good pictures in poor light. A basic model will cost £25-£30, but at that price it will not be automatic.

▲ A DISPOSABLE CAMERA

A disposable camera has the film sealed inside it. When you have used up the film, you simply hand over the camera to be developed. The photographs are returned to you, but the camera is re-cycled. You can use it to experiment with photography before deciding what kind of camera to buy.

SINGLE LENS REFLEX (SLR)

These cameras are very expensive but you may be lucky enough to be given a second-hand one, or be able to borrow one. This one belongs to the model's mother and is over 10 years old. SLR cameras usually have both automatic and manual controls and separate lenses for taking different kinds of pictures (see page 11).

ONE OFF WONDERS

There are a range of disposable cameras on the market today to cater for every kind of occasion.

◀ This 'one-use' camera has been specially designed for taking photographs in and under the water. An ideal choice for holidays on the beach.

▼ With a panoramic or wide angle 'one-use' camera you can get more of a scene into the frame of your photograph. A good choice for country and ski-ing holidays.

USING A CAMERA

All cameras have some basic features in common. To get the most from your camera, you should know what the main parts are called and what they do.

Illustrated here are the main parts on a fixed focus 35 mm compact camera.

Always keep your camera in a case when you are not using it.

SHUTTER RELEASE BUTTON
This is pressed when you want to take a photograph.

VIEWFINDER
The viewfinder shows you what the camera lens will be taking a picture of.

BUILT-IN FLASH
For taking a photograph when there is not enough light. See page 22.

FLASH BUTTON
To turn on flash.

SLIDING LENS CAP
Always keep the lens cap on when the camera is not in use to protect the lens.

SLIDING LENS CAP BUTTON
To open and close sliding lens cap.

FRONT VIEW

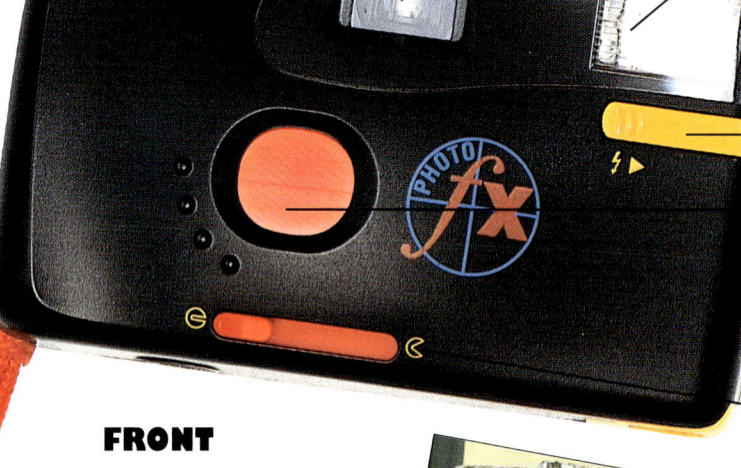

BACK OFF
If you are using a fixed focus camera don't get too near to your subject. You must be at least 1.5 metres away.

This girl got too close when taking a picture of her pet hamster. The camera has focused on to the background and not the hamster.

DOOR RELEASE BUTTON
To open the back of the camera to put in or take out film. NEVER open the back of the camera until the used film has been rewound into the cassette.

FLASH READY LIGHT
If there is not enough light to take a photograph, you will usually see a warning light when you look through the viewfinder. This tells you to turn on the flash. When the flash is ready to use the flash ready light will come on.

VIEWFINDER
When you look through the viewfinder you will usually see some framing marks. Anything you see inside those marks will appear on the final photograph.

FILM WIND ON
If your camera does not have automatic wind-on you will need to wind on the film yourself.

FILM CASSETTE HOLDER
To take pictures, a camera must be loaded with a film. You will find more information on the types of film you can buy on page 12.

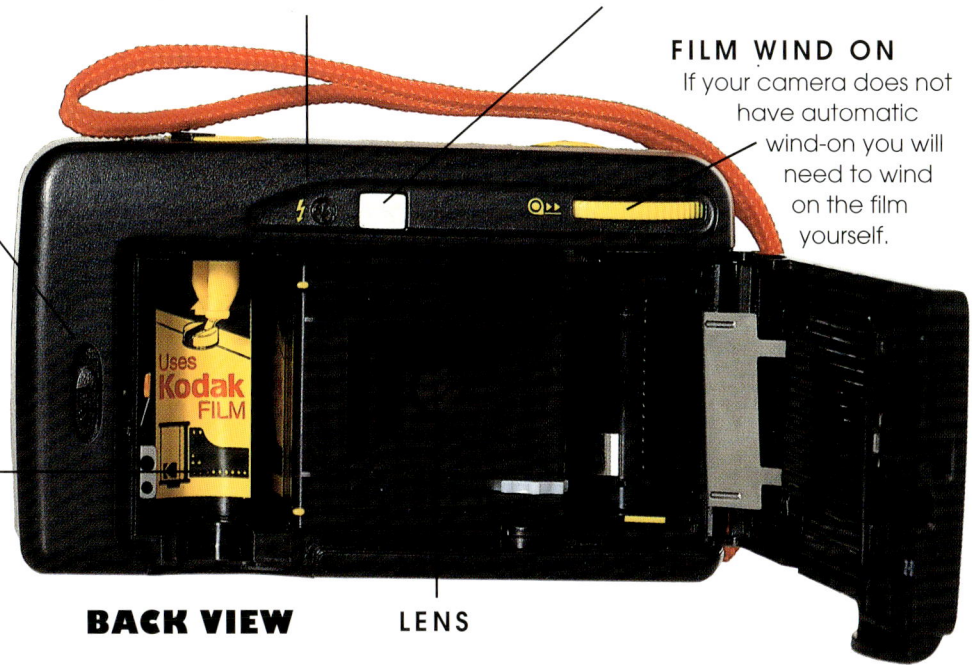

BACK VIEW   **LENS**

A WORD ABOUT SLR LENSES

Unlike most other cameras, an SLR camera can be fitted with different lenses. These photographs of two children in a hammock were taken at the same distance using the same camera, but each time the lens was changed. A lens has a 'focal length' which is measured in millimetres. This figure affects the area of a scene that a camera can fit into a photograph. The smaller the focal length measurement, the more that can be fitted into the frame as this sequence of photos clearly shows.

▶ Taken with a standard lens (focal length: 50 mm). This is the type of lens found in most cameras.

▼ Taken with a telephoto lens (focal length: 210 mm). This lens acts like a telescope, making the subject of your photograph appear much closer than it really is. In this picture we can no longer see that the children are sitting on a hammock.

◀ Taken with a wide angle lens (focal length: 28 mm). This type of lens is perfect for landscapes as it has a much wider angle of view than a standard lens.

▲ Taken with a long lens (focal length: 70 mm). The children can be seen in more detail.

WHICH FILM?

On these two pages you'll learn all about the types of film available and most importantly how to load film correctly.

TYPES OF FILM

▼ COLOUR NEGATIVE FILM
This is the most commonly used film, and therefore it is the cheapest to process. The colour negative film is developed into colour negatives which are then printed into colour photographs.

35 mm

CARTRIDGE

▲ BLACK AND WHITE
Black and white film is developed into black and white negatives which are then printed into black and white photographs. If you want to learn how to develop your own black and white film join a photography club that has darkroom facilities.

▲ COLOUR TRANSPARENCY FILM
Colour transparency film is processed into slides. To look at slides properly you need a projector to project the image on to a screen or a white wall. It is expensive to make prints from transparencies. Slide film gives very good results, but you must look after the slides very carefully.

FILM SIZE
Most cameras take 35 mm film. This is a measurement of the width of the film. 35 mm film comes in different lengths, and the length determines how many pictures you will get on to the film. The most common film lengths are 24 and 36.
The most common alternative to 35 mm film is 110 cartridge film. This type of film is used for the first camera featured on page 8. Do make sure that you buy the right type of film for your camera.

CARING FOR YOUR CAMERA
The two main causes of damage to cameras are:
Leaking Batteries: Always take out the batteries when you know that you won't be using your camera for more than a week.
Dust or Sand: Keep your camera clean by brushing it regularly with a blower brush. If you do not have one of these a clean pastry or make-up brush will do just as good a job.

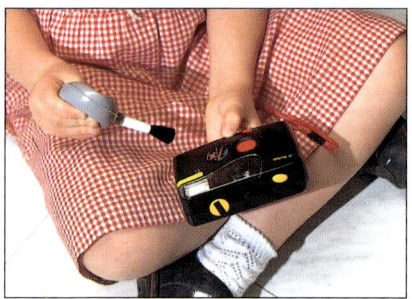

FILM SPEED

The boxes of cartridge and 35 mm films are marked with a number. This is called an ISO number and it indicates the speed with which the film reacts to light. The lower the number, the slower the film.

This photograph was taken indoors in poor light with a slow film – 100 ISO film. The results are very dark. Slow film is best used in situations where there is a lot of light: taking photographs outside on a bright sunny day, or for snow scenes, or when you will be using the flash a lot.

This photograph was taken under exactly the same lighting conditions but this time a faster film was used – 400 ISO film. The results are much better. Fast film is best used in situations where there is poor light: for taking photographs on a dull or overcast day or for night scenes.

LOADING THE FILM

Carefully follow the instructions that came with your camera for loading film. To check that the film has been correctly loaded, take one picture (which will be wasted) and wind on with the back still open. Once you are satisfied that the film is winding on, close the back and DO NOT OPEN again until you have used the film up and rewound it back into the cassette following the manufacturer's instructions.

To load this camera the rewind lever must be pulled up to insert the film cassette. Once the film is loaded, it is pressed down again to keep the cassette in place.

Enough film has been pulled out from the cassette to insert the end into the slot of the take-up spool.

If you run your finger along the holes at the bottom of the film you should be able to feel the notches poking through.

COMPOSING A PHOTOGRAPH

When you look through your camera's viewfinder you will see the scene that you are about to take a photograph of. Before taking the photograph, you should ask yourself whether what you can see can be improved upon to make a better picture. This is called composing a photograph. The information on the next four pages will help you to think about the compostion of the photographs you take.

THAT'S INTERESTING! ▶
This little girl is about to discover how important the compostion of a photograph is. It can make the difference between an ordinary photograph and a really interesting one.

▶ In her first photograph there is no main focus point. We are not drawn to any part of the photograph in particular – it is simply a penful of sheep.

▼ At her second attempt, she grabs our attention. She chooses to fill the frame with a mother and her lamb.

LANDSCAPE OR PORTRAIT?
The way you hold your camera when you take a photograph will affect the shape of the picture.

▲ If you turn the camera sideways you can take a vertical shot. This is also called a portrait photograph.

▶ If you hold your camera normally you will take a horizontal-shaped picture. This is also called a landscape and is particularly good for taking photographs of wide scenes.

A DISTANT VIEW ▶▼

Many landscape photographs end up looking flat and boring. To avoid this, you should try to lead the viewer into the picture. When you are composing the photograph, try to include lines running into the distance, such as a road for example.

THINKING BIG

It may be difficult to get a large building into the frame of a photograph. But you need not necessarily include the whole building in your picture to get an impression of its size or beauty.

◀ You've managed to squeeze the whole cathedral into the picture – well just about! Shame about the cut-off people in the foreground.

▲ Try to view the scene in a different way. If you point your camera upwards, you may not be able to get the whole building in the scene, but the photograph will give an impression of the cathedral's immense size.

◀ Or look for a detail on the building that will make an interesting photograph. Come in close and fill the frame.

▶ In this final photograph of the cathedral, the bush in the foreground helps to break up the blue sky and contains the picture.

Continued on next page

THE REAR VIEW

When you are taking a photograph of someone or something, it can be all too easy to forget about what is going on in the background. Don't! A distracting background can ruin a good photograph.

◀ An unfortunately composed photograph. The tree looks as if it is growing out of the subject's head.

▶ A carefully composed photograph. The subject of the photograph – the girls – are in the centre of the picture. The photographer has placed them against an attractive background – an arched red-brick wall that neatly frames them.

GRANNY'S GARDEN

These two portraits of granny show what a difference careful composition can make to a photograph.

▲ Although granny has been centrally positioned our attention is directed away from her. The window in the background is dull and boring, but its strong horizontal and vertical lines demand our attention. And the foreground is no better. A bush cuts across our view of granny.

▲ Here the photographer has taken a picture of granny as she looks out through her window. The window frames her and the garden scene reflected in the window glass creates a dramatic backdrop to the photograph.

▶ STABLE BOYS

One of the secrets of a well-composed photograph is not to go for the obvious shot. Instead of taking a picture of the children standing in front of the stable door, the photographer has them peeking over the stable door.

POINT OF VIEW

Don't take a photograph of a scene from the first angle you see. Try looking at it from several different view points before deciding which makes the best picture.

▶ A first picture taken on arrival at the beach. There is no depth to the photograph and no sense of scale.

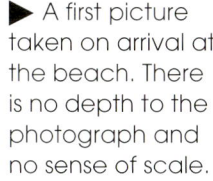

◀ This second snap is so much better. The donkeys being ridden along the beach draw our eye into the photograph. But how much better this picture would have been if the photographer had positioned herself so that the donkeys were being ridden towards her.

▼ These two pictures were taken from the same place, but one was taken under the water and the other when the photographer surfaced. Both pictures were taken with a one-use water-proof camera.

STREET VIEW

When you are thinking about the composition of your photograph you are trying to arrange the subject of your photograph in an interesting and effective way that will make people want to look at it.

▲ In the town, a view up the street can make an interesting alternative to a head on view of the local shops and houses.

▶ This café window with its white curtain and black frame makes a strong pattern.

LIGHTING A PHOTOGRAPH

It is impossible to take a photograph without light. If you with your camera are the artist with a brush and canvas, then light is the paint. And just as there are different types of paint there are different forms of light. If you want to take better photographs it is important to know how light can affect the pictures you take and how to make the best use of it.

EXPOSURE

When you take a photograph by pressing your finger down on the shutter release button, a shutter inside the camera opens to let light into the camera. The light travels through a hole inside the camera called an aperture to reach the film. The film is exposed when the light reaches it. The amount of light that reaches the film will depend on the size of the aperture and how long the shutter stays open.

◀ **CORRECTLY EXPOSED**
Just enough light reached the film and the photograph looks just as it did in real life.

OVEREXPOSED ▶
If too much light reaches the film the photograph will look too light.

◀ **UNDEREXPOSED**
If enough light does not reach the film the photograph will look too dark.

USE YOUR HEAD ... LIGHTS!

Why not try to take some night shots outside by using car headlights to light the photograph. Or why not try these other unusual lighting sources? Street lights; neon lights from shops or advertisements; fire light; torch light.

BATTERY POWER

Many cameras set the exposure automatically using an electronic cell on the front of the camera which is linked to an in-built light meter. The light meter measures the amount of light entering the camera and is powered by battery. So always make sure that you have spare batteries with you.

LET THERE BE LIGHT

You can light your photographs with natural light or artificial light or a combination of both. You will soon discover that different types of light produce different colours.

▶ This photograph was taken outside in the morning sun. Photographs taken in morning and midday sun have a blue tint.

◀ This photograph was lit with late afternoon sun coming in from the window which floods the photograph with a lovely yellow light.

▼ This photograph was lit by an anglepoise lamp which throws a golden yellow light over the two girls creating a warm and cosy atmosphere.

▶ Here daylight and electric house light have been combined to light the picture. Although the photograph was taken close to a window, the girl's face would have appeared much too dark if the lamp had not been turned on.

▲ Neon lighting is often found in offices, schools and shops. This type of lighting makes all white surfaces look green.

Continued on next page

Lighting a photograph continued

LOOKING AT LIGHT

To be able to take better photographs you must learn to make light work for you. Look at objects and observe how light can affect the way they appear. Pick something that you can see from your bedroom window, such as a tree in the garden, and take a look at it at different times of the day – first thing in the morning when you get out of bed, in the middle of the day, late in the afternoon, and last thing at night. Notice how the position of the sun in the sky throughout the day affects the way the shadows fall. Also notice how the weather can affect the quality of the light and change the atmosphere of a picture.

STUDY OF A TREE

The three pictures on this page are all of the same tree, and yet how different it looks in each. This was achieved by changing the angle that the photographs were taken from, and by taking the pictures at different times of the day and in varying weather conditions.

▲ This dramatic photograph was taken in cloudy, stormy weather.

▲ This photograph taken in bright sunny weather has strong colours and a feeling of depth.

◄ Backlighting can produce very dramatic landscape photographs at sunrise or sunset.

LIGHTING UP TIME

You can take a picture of something or someone with the light falling on it from three basic angles.

▼ FRONT LIGHTING

Light falls on the subject from the front. This is not very good for portrait shots (see page 33) as people narrow their eyes when looking into the sun and the light can make dark shadows under their eyes and nose.

A PRIZE PHOTOGRAPH

These two photographs show how important it is to think about how the light falls on your subject and the effect that this will produce.

▶ BACK LIGHTING

The subject is lit from behind. Be careful when taking a back lit photograph that you do not end up with an under-exposed photograph. To avoid this use fill-in flash (see page 23) or reflect the light back onto the subject (see page 33).

▼ When the sun is low in the sky front lighting will throw your shadow into the frame of the picture. If this happens take the photograph from a different position.

▼ By taking the photograph from this position the strong sunlight is falling on the back of the subject. Dark shadows cover her face completely.

▼ SIDE LIGHTING

This is when the light falls on the subject of your photograph from any other angle than directly in front or directly behind.

▲ By changing your position so that the light falls on the subject from the side the winning rider's face can be clearly seen as she proudly receives her rossette.

USING FLASH

If there is not enough light to take a photograph you will need to use the flash. On these two pages you will find out how to use flash effectively.

This camera has a built-in pop-up flash unit.

FINDING YOUR FLASH

Many cameras have a built in electronic flash unit (see page 10). How this works will depend on the type of camera you have. Some cameras automatically activate the flash when there is not enough light; some cameras make a high-pitched noise or flash a light in the viewfinder to let you know that you should turn on the flash; and with other cameras you have to judge for yourself whether there is enough light to take a good photograph.

FLASH POINT
NEVER use flash at public performances or sporting events as you may distract the performer.

GETTING CLOSER ...

Flash light is very bright, but even so if you stand too far from your subject the flash light won't be strong enough to light it up. If you are taking a night time photograph outdoors, the flash will only light up objects to a distance of about 15 metres.

▲...BUT NOT TOO CLOSE!

When taking photographs indoors, don't get too close to your subject or you may overexpose her. For the best results, your subject should be 1-3 metres from the camera.

▲ You can use flash to take a picture of a building outdoors.

▲ Flash will let you get quite a lot of the building in the photograph.

▶ Flash will provide enough light to take a photograph of the building up to a distance of 15 metres.

▼ Beyond 15 metres the flash will not provide enough light to light up the building.

FILL-IN FLASH

You can also use flash outdoors during the day to soften shadows cast by strong sunlight.

Strong overhead sunlight causes the rider's hat to throw hard shadows across her face.

By using the flash, you can 'fill-in' hard shadows.

A BIRTHDAY CELEBRATION

Flash will come in very useful when you want to record a special occasion such as a birthday party, if you remember to follow a few simple rules.

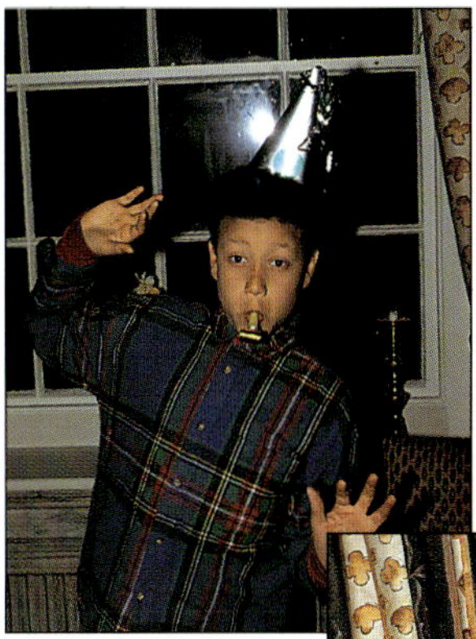

LINE THEM UP

In this photograph some of the guests are too light and some are too dark. This is because the flash has measured itself to the child nearest the camera and those further away have been underexposed.

THE BIRTHDAY BOY

Flash light will reflect back into the camera if you have a reflective surface, such as a glass window or mirror, behind your subject.

◀ Here the problem was solved by simply drawing the curtains.

▶ **FLASH FIENDS**
If you do not use flash with care, the results can be very unflattering! Hard shadows thrown by flash and 'red-eye' can be overcome by diffusing the light. You can do this by covering the flash with tissue or tracing-paper.

▶ **GUEST GATHERING**
To get a correctly exposed photograph try to keep all the birthday guests the same distance from the camera.

COMMON MISTAKES

It is always very exciting seeing the prints from your developed film for the first time. Sadly, you may not always end up with the results that you had hoped for. Here are some dos and don'ts to help you avoid the most common mistakes.

▲ **Don't** get your finger in front of the lens.

▼ **Do** wind on your film correctly to avoid fogging the first photograph (see page 13). And don't forget to carry a spare film with you in case you run out!

◀ **Don't** let your hair get in front of the camera. If you've got long hair, it's a good idea to tie it back on breezy days.

▶ **Do** make sure there is enough light to take your photograph. If necessary use your flash. If the flash on your camera is battery powered, don't forget to carry a spare battery with you.

▶ **Do** make sure that the camera is focusing on the subject of the photograph. Auto focus cameras will focus on whatever is in the centre of the viewfinder, in this case the foliage. To avoid this you must use the focus lock. Point the camera at the main subject of the photograph, in this case the butterfly. Press the shutter release button half way down. Now move the camera so that you can see everything that you want to take a picture of in the viewfinder and press down the shutter release button fully.

◀ **Don't** fidget. Keep yourself and the camera very still when you are taking a photograph, otherwise you will end up with a blurred image.

DO LOOK AFTER YOUR CAMERA

Always keep your camera in a case when you are not using it. You can make your own from an old padded envelope, decorated with cut up photographs.

▲ **Don't** forget your camera! Always carry your camera with you wherever you go. You never know when you will spot something worth photographing.

OUT IN THE COUNTRY

The countryside can be a great place to find interesting subjects. But before you take a photograph of a scene take a good look at it. Are you really getting the best possible picture? On the next few pages you'll find some tips to help you.

A DIFFERENT VIEW

Don't always take the obvious photograph. Have a go at taking pictures from different angles.

▶ Lie down on the grass to get a close-up view of a group of daffodils.

▶ Try pointing your camera upwards to look through the branches of a tree, but do make sure that the sunlight is not pointing directly into the camera lens.

A FOCUSED VIEW

When taking a close-up view of your subject, do make sure that you don't get so close that your camera cannot focus on it.

▼ A fixed focus camera will not focus on subjects that are less than 1.5 metres away. Here the camera has focused on the background, leaving the subject of the photograph – the crocuses – blurry.

◀ To get a close up view of the crocuses you will need to use a camera that has an adaptable focus, such as an SLR.

THE RIGHT MOMENT

When you are taking a photograph, the time of day and the weather conditions may have an important part to play. If you choose your moment carefully you can get some beautiful results.

MAKING A COLLAGE

Take lots of close up photographs on your day out in the country and use them to make a collage. Cut around your favourite images and arrange them on to thick card. Glue in place. You could also make a collage of holiday snaps.

▲ This photograph was taken at dawn on a frosty spring morning.

◀ This photograph was taken after it had been raining and the trees are glistening.

A DAY AT THE BEACH

If you take your camera to the beach with you, you can end up with some very interesting photographs. But do take care. Sand and sea can damage your camera.

I SEE THE SEA
When you are taking a picture of the sea, don't just point your camera towards the horizon line. Stop and think about what you are taking a photograph of.

▼ By trying to capture the whole scene you may end up with a very boring picture with no sense of scale.

▶ In this photograph we can see the shoreline as well as the sea. The dog and the couple walking in the distance help to give a feeling of depth to the picture.

◀ A CHANGE OF VIEW
So think carefully about what you can see in the viewfinder. Try out different viewpoints until you find a part of the scene that is worth taking a photograph of. In this photograph the breakwaters in the foreground help to break up the view and give a sense of scale.

▶ HOMING IN
A closer view of the breakwater can also produce an interesting photograph.

▶ Record the shapes and colours of the pebbles.

▼ Frame the action of the sea on a breakwater.

ON THE SHORE LINE
Instead of pointing the camera straight ahead, look up, down and around.

▼ Photograph the drift washed up by the sea.

▲ Capture the foam as it breaks on the beach.

TAKING CARE OF YOUR CAMERA
The beach can be a very dangerous place for your camera so do take extra special care of it.

Don't get sand in your camera. It will destroy the inner workings. For this reason, never change the film while you are on the beach.

Don't get your camera wet. Pack your camera in a plastic bag when you are not using it.

Don't lay your camera in direct sunlight as excessive heat will ruin the film. Make sure it is in a shady place when you are not using it.

OUT AND ABOUT IN THE TOWN

A walk through your local town will provide you with lots of inspiration for taking photographs. But if you don't know where to begin, here are some ideas to start you off.

◀ SHOES GALORE
A display of goods in a shop window can make a colourful picture. But do be careful of reflections. Make sure that you take the photographs from an angle where there are no reflections.

OUR HOUSE
You can make a panoramic photograph of the street in which you live. Make sure you take each photograph from exactly the same distance from the houses. Try to have your camera on a tripod if you can, as it is important that the camera is at the same height for every picture. You could also take this street scene with a disposable wide-angle or panoramic camera.

My Room!

▲ MAKING A MARK
Rather than photographing subjects that can be found in any town, try to find things that are special to your town, like a monument, a fountain, or a statue.

LOCAL EVENTS

Keep a look out in the local newspaper for fêtes and craft fairs. These can offer good subjects for your photographs.

▲ FOR SALE
A display of stall holder's wares at a local fête can make an interesting picture.

TREASURE HUNT
For a birthday outing with a difference, why not organise a photographic treasure hunt. Divide the party guests into three or four teams. Each team will

need a camera loaded with a roll of film. Ask an adult to make out the list of objects and to be the independent judge of the competition. Give each team an identical list of things that they must photograph, for example: a bicycle, a mop, a green door, a ginger cat, someone blowing up a balloon, a number 8, and so on. They then have one hour to go off and take those pictures. By the end of the hour, all the teams must return to base (any latecomers are disqualified). Dad then takes the films to a one-hour processing lab while everyone tucks into tea. The processed photographs are judged for number of subjects taken and the inventiveness of the shot.

FACE PAINTING
When recording events at a local event, try to tell a story with your photographs.

▶ Cor that's good! I wish I could have my face painted.

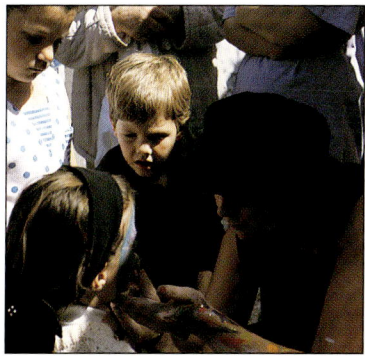

◀ Yeah – it's my turn now.

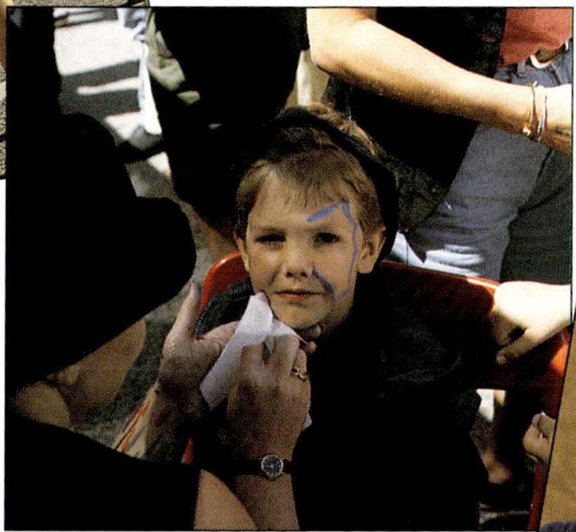

▲ DANCING GIRLS
A troupe of dancers at a village summer fair makes a colourful subject for a photograph.

▶ Well – what do you think?

PHOTOGRAPHING A PERSON

When you first begin photography you will probably want to take lots of photographs of your family and friends. Taking photographs of people is called portrait photography. On the next few pages there are some tips for taking good portrait photographs. First you need a willing subject – ask Mum if she can spare a few minutes. If it is a sunny day, take the photograph outside in the garden or even at the local park.

OFF WITH HER HEAD! ▶
Don't stand too near your subject or you will risk cutting off her head!

◀ WHERE IS SHE?
But don't stand too far away either. The viewfinder on your camera (see page 10) will show you exactly what is being seen by the camera lens.

THE BACKGROUND STORY
Do think about what you can see behind the person you are photographing. An untidy background is very distracting and not very flattering.

BITS AND PIECES
Always save your mistakes. You can have great fun with them. You could make a wacky mixed up family album. Begin by sticking Dad's head on Mum's body!

GETTING THE LIGHTING RIGHT

Taking photographs in natural sunlight can give the best results – if you keep to a few simple rules.

SUN IN HER EYES ▶
Make sure that the person you are photographing is not sitting facing the sun. The sun going in her eyes will make her squint and her skin may look shiny.

DIRECT SUN IN THE LENS ▶
But don't position your subject with her back to the sun. The sun will be shining directly into the camera lens and will make the photograph look bleached out.

HARD SHADOWS ▶
Position the person so that the sun is coming in from the side. However, if the sunlight is very strong, it can make hard shadows on the nose and under the eyes and chin.

PERFECTION!
The perfect portrait picture. Remember: don't stand too close or too faraway; choose an uncluttered background; and try to reflect strong sunlight onto the face of your subject. ▼

A TOWEL REFLECTOR
Avoid hard shadows by reflecting the sunlight off a white surface and onto the person's face. Use a towel draped over a chair.

KEEP IT RELAXED

When you are taking a photograph of someone you will get the best results if she is feeling relaxed and comfortable.

SMILE PLEASE!
It's hard to look natural when someone points a camera at you and tells you to smile. Although granny is smiling here, her tense shoulders and clasped hands tell us she is feeling far from relaxed.

AT HOME
The results are so much better when granny is feeling at home in a comfortable chair with her dog for company.

PHOTOGRAPHING A BABY

As any professional photographer will tell you, it's not easy to get a good photograph of a baby. For the best results, always try to take a picture of baby with his Mum or Dad.

▶ HELLO MUM!
Now here's a face he recognises! But although you've got a photo of baby smiling, you've also got the back of Mum's head! You could make an enlargement of the photo from the negative and crop out mum's head (see page 46).

▲ WHO ARE YOU?
Until a baby is old enough to sit up by himself, the only way to take a photograph of him is when he is lying on his back. This makes him look very odd. And it's very unlikely that he will smile at you, because your face is hidden by the camera.

◀ MOTHER AND BABY
Although he's not smiling, baby is perfectly relaxed in Mum's arms and his face can be clearly seen. When he is grown up this baby will treasure this photograph.

SURPRISE! SURPRISE!

You can often get the most natural results when taking a photograph of someone if they do not know that you are about to take their picture. But be careful that you do not make them jump, particularly if they are carrying something that could break easily

HIDE AWAY
Find a place to hide where you can see the person coming, but they can't see you.

DAYDREAMER
This unsuspecting subject has no idea that she is about to have her photograph taken.

GOTCHA!
As she realises you are there, take a photograph quickly. The results are naturally animated.

RESPECT PEOPLE'S PRIVACY
Most people say that they hate having their photo taken, so to take the best photographs of your family and friends you may need to arrange a surprise like this. But if you want to take a photograph of a person you don't know, on holiday for example, do ask first. They will quite likely be flattered and pleased. Always make sure you send them a copy of the picture if they ask for one.

GROUP PHOTOGRAPHS

Photographing more than one person at a time can present you with a few problems. How should you best position them? How can you keep their attention long enough to take a good photograph? On the next few pages there are lots of ideas for taking interesting photographs of groups of people.

▲ A FAMILY OCCASION
A family gathers to celebrate the first birthday of a child. Everyone stands grouped around Grandmother who is seated holding the birthday boy. This gives a central point of interest to the photograph.

◄ A DAY AT THE BEACH
This holiday snap works well because of the bright colours and the position of the children. Although everyone isn't smiling and some of the faces are quite grumpy it's a happy picture nevertheless.

HEAD TO HEAD
This photograph of a grandmother with her grandchild is successful because they have been positioned so that their heads are at different levels. The photograph has been taken close to a window for natural light. The window light was reflected back onto the faces of the people by draping a white towel over a chair back (see page 33). ▶

A SWIMMING PARTY ▲
This is an example of a group photograph that does not work. The photographer is too far away, so that the end product is a picture of the swimming pool rather than the people in it.

BIKERS ▶

In this informal group photograph of a mother and her three daughters the children's red sweaters and the afternoon sun give the picture a warm golden glow.

◀ HEAD SHOTS

A breakwater at the beach gave the perfect opportunity for taking a very unusual group photograph of friends.

RUN PLEASE ▶

For an action picture try taking a photograph of a group of friends rushing towards you.

◀ A FAMILY NIGHT IN

It's not always easy to persuade older brothers and sisters to pose for a photograph. You may find that you get the best results if you catch them off guard – when they're watching tv for example!

DOS AND DON'TS

Do have a plan in mind of where you want each person to stand – it can even be a good idea to sketch out a seating plan beforehand so that everyone does not get bored waiting for you to decide where they should go.

Don't get annoyed if someone won't do what you ask him to. Try asking him to work out a difficult sum (22 x 108 for example). That should distract him for long enough for you to take the picture.

Do make sure that everyone can see the lens of the camera. Move people around until everyone can see the lens.

Don't say smile! The results will look unnatural. Try to relax everyone by telling a joke, or singing a song.

Do take lots of photographs. If you've gone to all that trouble to get everyone together, you should give yourself plenty of choice.

PHOTOGRAPHING SCHOOL FRIENDS

As any school photographer will tell you, it's very difficult to get a good photograph of a large group of children. Often there are as many as 20 or 30 children in the class and everyone has to be carefully positioned, usually in rows, so that each child's face can be clearly seen. And there's usually at least one person who had his eyes shut or looked away when the photograph was taken! If you want to photograph a large group of your school friends, you may have better luck with one of these ideas.

CLASS LINE UP

You will find that it is much easier to take a photograph of a small group of people. First choose a plain background, such as a stonebrick wall. Line up a group of three friends against the background and take their picture. Now line up another three, and take their picture, then another three, and so on, until you have photographed the whole class.

ALL TOGETHER

When the photographs are developed, choose your favourites. Now you can start to join your friends together. Take one print and cut around the outline of the end child. Stick this on top of the next print, so that the children look as if they are standing next to each other. Carry on in this way with the other prints.

HEADS OF THE CLASS

To make a class collage like this, take a photograph of each of your friends. Try to keep the top of their heads in the photograph or you may end up with a few flat heads. When the photographs are developed, cut out their heads and stick them all together. If you are using a fixed focus camera (see page 9), you will need to send your film to a company that can produce giant prints for you or the heads will be too small to cut out.

HEADS TOGETHER

▲ LOOKING UP

Get everyone to lie down with their heads together. Climb on to a small step ladder and take their picture from above.

▶ You will need to use your flash for this picture, even if you are taking it outdoors on a sunny day. So many heads crowded around above you will block out the light.

▼ LOOKING DOWN

Or you can lie on the floor and get everyone to crowd around above you. If possible, ask long-haired friends to tie back their hair. Make sure everyone can see the camera lens.

TRICK PHOTOS

Now that you have learnt how to take a good picture and how to avoid the most commonly made mistakes, you can start to have some real fun. On the next few pages you're going to find out how to take photographs that will truly amaze your friends.

A HEAVY BURDEN

Get an adult to stand on a stool with his arms outstretched as if he is balancing. The child should crouch in front, so that the stool's legs are hidden. Ask the child to put her hands palm-facing up onto her shoulders, and to look as if she is holding something very heavy.

A HAIR RAISING EXPERIENCE

You will need the help of someone with longish hair. This trick will not work with a short-haired person. Get your friend to hang upside down (from a park swing or climbing frame) with her arms folded across her chest. Take her picture. When the photograph is developed simply turn it upside down.

41

MONSTER FACE
Take this picture indoors after dark so that there is not too much light around. Dress your friend in a black top and stand her up against a dark background. Shine a light upwards from underneath her face. Ask her to pull a frightening face as you take her photograph.
NOTE: If your camera has an automatic flash this trick will not work unless you remove the battery first.

FOUR ARMS
You need the help of two friends for this one. Get them both to wear the same coloured tops. Ask one friend to stand behind the other with his arms around her waist. You must not be able to see his body or head. Have each of the four arms doing something, as in this photo.

BALANCING ACT
Find a wall or a pillar that is about the same height as your friend. Put a vase of flowers on it and line up your friend so that his head is just underneath the vase.

PHOTOGRAPHING ANIMALS

You will find that taking a photograph of an animal is very different from photographing people. For one thing you can be sure that an animal will act completely naturally, which may not always be a good thing. For example, you may be ready to take a photograph of your dog when he decides it's time to chase your next door neighbour's cat instead! To get good results you will need to take your time. But if you are patient you will get some great pictures. Here are some tips to help you.

Always keep your camera handy and be ready to capture those special pictures.

DEALING WITH DOGS

You will get much better results if you take a photograph of a dog together with her owners. She will be much less likely to run off and the results will be relaxed and happy.

LYING DOGGO

It can be difficult to take a good photograph of your own dog. As soon as he sees you pointing a camera at him, he will probably want to come to you. Try climbing up into a small tree and then call his name. This way, you make sure that he keeps his distance from you while you take his picture.

To get his full attention try calling "Miaow" a few times!

CAPTURING CATS

Cats are very photogenic, which means that generally they look good in photographs. But, as any cat owner will tell you, cats can't be told what to do. So you will need to stalk a cat as if it is a wild animal, and be ready to 'shoot' when it least expects it.

This cat has been startled by the photographer which makes her look very alert. You will have to work quickly to capture the moment before the cat slinks off to find a quiet corner.

◀ This black cat has the sunshine lighting up its black fur and green eyes. Always take a photograph of a black animal in good strong light, otherwise all the detail in its coat will be lost.

▼ LITTLE AND LARGE

Photographs taken of pets with their owners are often the most successful. Your photograph can capture a special relationship.

▲ WATCH THE BIRDIE!

If you have a bird table in your garden close to a window, try to take a photograph of birds as they feed off it. Don't try to take pictures of birds flying in the sky, unless you want a photo of black dots on a blue background!

ACTION!

If you are trying to take a picture of someone when he or she is moving vey fast, it is possible that the photograph may come out as a blur. Although this may give the impression of speed, it may also make it difficult to see what is going on. On these two pages you will learn how to control the movement captured on a photograph.

▼ FLAPPER
This photograph of a girl running was taken in poor lighting conditions on a dull, overcast day. But the result is quite effective.

FLASH IN THE PAN
In poor lighting conditions, indoors in artificial light for example, flash can be used to freeze movement.

▲ When using flash do be careful that the flash light is not reflected in glass.

▼ When no flash is used the result is very blurred.

▲ DANCING ON THE BEACH
A child dances with her father on the beach. The moment is frozen in time because the photographer has used a fast film (see page 13) and taken the picture in strong sunlight.

▲ PANNING

With a panned shot the background will appear blurry giving an impression of speed while the moving subject is clearly focused. This can be difficult to achieve, but remember practice makes perfect.

Holding your camera very firmly, follow the moving subject through the lens just as if you were using a video camera. Continue to follow him for a couple of seconds after you have taken the photograph.

JUMP FOR IT

Picture your friends from a completely different angle with this unusual way to take their photograph. Lie on the ground and get them to jump over you, and take their photograph as they do so.

◄ THE FINISHING WORD

Timing is essential when taking action photographs. Do make sure that you are in the right place at the right time to capture that winning shot.

WHAT NEXT?

The fun doesn't stop once you've taken the photos; here are some useful tips to help you get the most from your photographs.

GETTING YOUR FILM DEVELOPED

Before developing your film, do a little research to find out which company is offering the best deal.

You can choose between gloss or matt prints. If you intend to frame any of the prints behind glass ask for a matt finish as a gloss finish will be too reflective.

▲ STARTING A NEGATIVE FILE

To keep track of your photographs it is a good idea to start a negative file. You never know, one day your photographs could be worth a fortune!

Put each set of negatives into a separate envelope, then number and date the envelope. In a notebook enter the details for each envelope of negatives: the number on the envelope, the date, and a brief description of the pictures. Keep the notebook and the negative envelopes in a box. Mark the back of each print with the corresponding envelope number. If you do this, you will always be able to find the negative of a print from the number written on its back, should you need to have another print made.

▲ CROPPING A PHOTOGRAPH

Many photographs can be improved by cropping – that is cutting away any unwanted bits and leaving behind a selected area. To do this, cut two 15cm-wide L-shapes from cardboard. Lay the two L's across one another on top of the photograph.

Try moving the L shapes around until you find the perfect picture. Use a sharp pencil to mark this on to the print and cut along the pencil lines.

If you would like the image made larger, get the whole negative enlarged and crop it yourself.

GLOSSARY

Angle of view The amount of a scene that a camera can fit into a photo. This will vary depending on the focal length of the lens.

Aperture A hole inside the camera surrounded by a circle of moveable metal blades which can be moved to adjust the size of the hole. The aperture size combined with shutter speed controls the amount of light reaching the film.

Auto focus A beam of infra-red light is bounced off a subject in front of the camera lens. This measures the distance of the subject and adjusts the camera's focus accordingly.

Composition The arrangement of people and objects within the scene that you want to photograph.

Developing A process that makes an image appear on film or on photographic paper.

Diffuser A transparent material, such as muslin or tracing or tissue-paper, placed in front of a direct source of light such as flash that spreads the light out and softens its effect. When you are taking a photograph of someone sitting by a window, a net curtain can help diffuse the light.

Exposure This is the amount of light that reaches the film in the camera and is controlled by the speed of the shutter and the size of the aperture.

Fill-in flash Using flash outdoors to soften the shadows produced by strong sunlight.

Film A specially-coated material which when exposed to light records what can be seen by the camera lens.

Film speed Different films react to light at different speeds. The speed of a film is measured by an ISO number.

Flash An artificial means of producing light when there is not enough light to take a photograph. A flash unit can be built into the camera or it can be a detachable unit.

Focal length This is the measurement of the distance needed between a camera lens and the film so that a distant object can be sharply focused. The focal length of a lens is measured in millimetres.

Focusing Moving the camera lens backwards or forwards to make the image appear sharp.

ISO number ISO stands for International Standards Organization and this is a system for measuring film speeds. The higher the number the faster the film.

Lens A curved glass or plastic disc that bends light rays coming into the camera so that they make an image on the film.

Light meter This measures the amount of light coming from the subject. It is usually built into the camera.

Negative When an exposed film is developed into a negative the image appears as the opposite of the final prints. The light parts appear dark and the dark parts appear transparent.

Panning A technique used to capture action on film. The photographer swings the camera around to keep a moving subject in the viewfinder, taking the photograph as she moves.

Printing Transferring an image from film on to light-sensitive paper to make a photograph.

Red-eye This is when the subject of your photograph appears to have flaming red eyes. It is most likely to happen when you are trying to take a photograph using flash when there is not enough light. It is caused because the iris of the eye is wide open and the flash lights up the blood vessels inside the eye. It can be avoided by turning on an additional light source such as an overhead light.

Shutter When you press the shutter release button to take a photograph a shutter behind the camera lens opens to let light through. How much light reaches the film is affected by the speed with which the shutter opens and shuts.

Single lens reflex (SLR) This type of camera is named after its special 'reflex' viewfinding system. Light coming through the lens is bounced off a 'reflex' mirror system so that the viewfinder and the lens receive the same image.

Viewfinder This allows you to see what can be seen by the camera lens, so that you can compose your photograph. In all cameras except SLRs, the scene through the viewfinder differs very slightly from the one seen through the lens. This will only cause a problem on close-up shots.

Wide angle lens A lens with a short focal length (28 mm) that has a much wider angle of view than an ordinary lens and therefore is useful for taking a photograph of a wide scene.

INDEX

A
action photographs 37, 44-5
angle of view 47
animals, photographing 7, 42-3
aperture 18, 47

B
baby, photographing a 34
background 16, 32, 33, 38
battery 5, 12, 18, 24

C
camera 8-11
  automatic 8
  caring for 29
  case 25
  cleaning 12
  disposable 9
  fixed focus 9, 10, 26, 29
  110 camera 8
  single lens reflex (SLR) 9, 11, 26, 47
  35mm 9, 10
close ups 26
collage 27, 39
compostion 14-17, 47
cropping 34, 46

D
depth of photograph 17, 28
developing 46, 47
diffuser 47

E
enlargements 34
exposure 8, 18, 47
  automatic 8
  overexposure 18
  underexposure 18, 23

F
film 5, 8, 9, 11, 12-13, 18, 31, 47
  black and white 12
  cartridge 8, 12
  colour negative 12
  colour transparency 12
  loading 13, 14
  rewinding 8, 11, 13
  speed 13, 44, 47
  35mm 12
  winding on 8, 11, 13
flash 8, 9, 10, 11, 22-3, 24, 47
  auto 8, 41
  fill-in 21, 23, 47
  range 22, 23
  ready light 11
focal length 11, 47
focus 25, 26, 47
  automatic 8, 25, 47
  minimum focusing distance 10
focus of interest 14, 36
fogging 24
framing device 15, .16

G
group photos 7, 36-9

I
ISO numbers 13, 47

L
landscape photos 14
lens 9, 10, 32, 37, 39, 47
  cap 10
  long 11
  telephoto 11
  wide angle 11, 47
lighting 6, 18-21, 33, 43
  artificial 19, 41, 44, 47
  at different times of day 19, 20
  back 21

lighting continued
  front 21
  meter 47
  natural 19, 33, 36, 37
  neon 18, 19
  side 21

N
negative 34, 46, 47
  file 46

P
panning 45, 47
panoramic photograph 30
portrait photographs 7, 14, 32-5
prints 46, 47
  gloss 46
  matt 46
privacy 35
processing 31

R
red eye 23, 47
reflector 21, 33, 36

S
sense of scale 28
shutter 18, 47
  release 10.18, 25

T
taking photographs
  at the beach 28-9
  in the country 26-7
  in the town 30-31
take up spool 13
trick photographs 40-41

V
viewfinder 10, 11, 14, 22, 25, 28, 32, 47
viewpoint 17, 28